# Shiva Tales

An imprint of Om Books International

Published in 2014 by

An imprint of Om Books International

Corporate & Editorial Office
A 12, Sector 64, Noida 201 301
Uttar Pradesh, India
Phone: +91 120 477 4100
Email: editorial@ombooks.com
Website: www.ombooksinternational.com

Sales Office
4379/4B, Prakash House, Ansari Road
Darya Ganj, New Delhi 110 002, India
Phone: +91 11 2326 3363, 2326 5303
Fax: +91 11 2327 8091
Email: sales@ombooks.com
Website: www.ombooks.com

Retold by Subhojit Sanyal
Illustrations: Braj Kishore, Jithin, Naveen

ISBN: 978-93-82607-77-9

Printed at EIH Press, Gurgaon, India

10 9 8 7 6 5 4 3 2 1

# Contents

# THE GREATEST GOD IN THE UNIVERSE

One day, Lord Brahma and Lord Vishnu got into a heated argument. They both claimed to be the greatest god in the Universe. Lord Brahma said, "I have created everything on earth thus, I am the most powerful god." Lord Vishnu replied, "But I am the preserver of all your creations. Thus, I am the greatest."

As they continued arguing, a fiery lingam erupted from the earth between them. It stretched higher, without any end in sight. Both Lord Vishnu and Lord Brahma stared at it, trying to figure out its origin and end.

They both decided to find it out for themselves, and wagered that they will figure out the mystery before the other one. Lord Vishnu transformed into a wild boar and started digging into the earth to find the lingam's origins. Lord Brahma transformed himself into a swan and flew up to find its end.

Lord Vishnu went on digging into the earth, but was unable to find the lingam's origins. He gave up and emerged from the earth, defeated. Lord Brahma flew high, but was nowhere near finding the top end of the lingam. He saw a *ketaki* flower on his way, and carried it in his beak, back to earth.

He met Lord Vishnu and showed him the flower, claiming that he saw it on top of the lingam.

Suddenly, the sky reverberated with thunderstorms, and Lord Shiva came forth from the lingam. He pointed at Lord Brahma and said, "You are lying! Because of the sin, I curse you that no one will worship you, celebrate your festivals or build your temples." He further banished the use of *ketaki* flower from being used in his worship.

He turned to Lord Vishnu and said, "You have been honest and humble. Thus, you shall be worshipped, festivals will be celebrated in your honour and temple will be built for you on earth."

Lord Brahma was ashamed of his act, and asked for forgiveness. He and Lord Vishnu bowed down in front of Lord Shiva, conceding defeat and accepting Lord Shiva as the greatest god in the Universe.

# GANGA

Once the king of Ayodhya, King Sagara, was worried as he had no heirs. Along with his two wives, he went to Mount Kailash to perform severe penances. Soon, Lord Shiva appeared before them and blessed the king. He said, "You shall have sixty thousand sons from one wife, but they will all perish. Your other wife will have one boy, but his descendants will bring glory to your dynasty."

The king, with his queens, returned to kingdom. As predicted, one queen gave birth to sixty thousand sons, who grew up to be very brave warriors. The other queen gave birth to one son who grew up with his brothers to be a warrior like them.

After a few years, King Sagara decided to conduct the *Ashwamedha yagna* (ritual scarifice) to expand his kingdom. It was a ritual where a horse was released to wander for a year and the kings of all the kingdoms where the horse wandered were asked to submit to his rule or face war. Lord Indra, the King of the Devas, grew concerned as he feared that the horse will enter the heaven, and the king will easily defeat him. Therefore, he stole the ceremonial horse and tied it outside Sage Kapila's ashram.

When the horse could not be found, King Sagara sent his sixty thousand sons to find the horse. They turned the earth inside out in search for the horse. Finally, they reached Sage Kapila's ashram and found it. Assuming that the sage had stolen the horse, they threatened him, who was meditating. The sage opened his eyes and burned the princes to ashes with one glance.

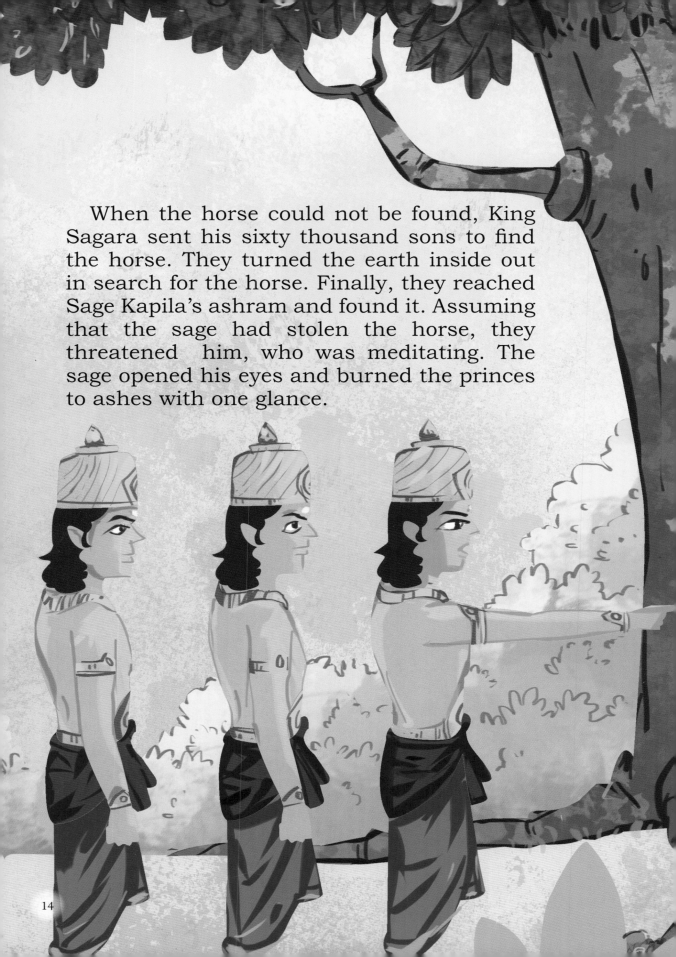

Anxious King Sagara, sent his grandson Anshuman to search for his uncles. He found the horse and his uncles' ashes outside Sage Kapila's ashram. He politely enquired about his uncles'. Sage Kapila was impressed by his humility and said, "They committed a fatal mistake. Only the purifying water of Goddess Ganga will help them attain heaven." A distraught Anshuman returned to King Sagara to deliver the news. The king was devastated by the news and decided to perform severe penance to Goddess Ganga. He passed away before his wish could be granted.

Anshuman succeeded King Sagara on throne, who was then followed by his grandson, Bhagiratha. Bhagiratha, like his grandfather and great-grandfather, performed severe penance to Goddess Ganga to fulfill his familial duties. Goddess Ganga heard his prayer but feared that her strong currents will wash away even the strongest gods. Lord Shiva assured her that he will see to it that her currents be tamed, and wound her up in his matted locks. But, not one drop of water fell on earth.

Bhagiratha grew concerned and decided to perform penance to Lord Shiva. Appeased by his devotion, Lord Shiva allowed Ganga to pour out from his locks, on earth. The water released Bhagiratha's ancestors, helping them to be in heaven.

# SHIVA AND SATI

Daksha, Lord Brahma's wish-born son, a *prajapati* (Lord of creatures), was entrusted with the duty to populate the Universe. He with his wife, Prastuti, had many daughters who were married off to gods and sages. Sati, his youngest daughter, was his favourite.

Sati was the reincarnation of Ardhashakti, or the better half of Lord Shiva which he had sacrificed to maintain the balance in the Universe and was thus, destined to marry Lord Shiva. But Daksha detested him and his hermetic lifestyle.

Sati grew up to be the most beautiful maiden in the entire Universe, and there were innumerable suitors who wanted her hand in marriage.

Sati, determined to fulfil her destiny, went to the Himalayas to meditate and appease Lord Shiva. Pleased with her devotion, he agreed to marry her at once.

All the gods attended their wedding. Daksha did not approve of the marriage, but reluctantly gave his consent. After the wedding, Lord Shiva and Goddess Sati made Mount Kailash their abode and led a happy married life.

Daksha felt insulted as he had to accept a hermetic Lord Shiva as his son-in-law and decided to avenge his pride. Soon after, he organised a grand *yagna* (ritual sacrifice) and invited all the gods except Lord Shiva.

When Goddess Sati found out about the *yagna*, she was furious at her father. She requested Lord Shiva to partcipate in it, but he refused. Goddess Sati was determined to confront her father. She said, "I am his daughter, and he owes me an explaination. He cannot stop me from being welcomed to my own home." Lord Shiva, sensing trouble, tried to stop Goddess Sati, but she would not listen to any warning.

When Goddess Sati arrived at her father's house, Daksha welcomed her coldly. He then proceeded to insult her husband in front of the guests.

Enraged at her father's behaviour, a furious Goddess Sati declared that she would not tolerate any insult of her husband. Invoking a sacrificial fire, Goddess Sati immolated herself and was reduced to ashes.

Lord Shiva was furious after learning about Sati's death. Unable to control his anger, he brought forth superior beings Virabhadra and Bhadrakali, to behead Daksha. Even though many gods tried to help Daksha, Virabhadra and Bhadrakali destroyed his army and beheaded him.

Lord Brahma pleaded to Lord Shiva for his son's life and asked for forgiveness for his behaviour. Lord Shiva calmed down, and revived Daksha by replacing his head with a goat's head. He placed Goddess Sati's body on his shoulder and started walking through the Universe, neglecting his duties. The gods were very concerned and approached Lord Vishnu to help restore balance in the Universe.

Lord Vishnu used his *sudarshan chakra* (a celestial weapon) to cut Sati's body to pieces, which fell on earth. Lord Shiva returned to Mount Kailash to meditate and mourn his wife's death. Goddess Sati eventually returned to Lord Shiva by taking birth as Parvati.

# SHIVA AND PARVATI

Goddess Sati took birth again on earth as the daughter of King Himavat and Queen Mena. They named her Parvati. Narad Muni came to look at the baby and declared she is destined to marry Shiva. While growing up, she would lose herself thinking about Lord Shiva.

When she was of marriageable age, she went to the Himalayas to perform penance and appease Lord Shiva and marry him. Lord Shiva was impressed by her devotion and knew about her desire, but he was still in mourning for Goddess Sati. He asked Parvati to serve him as the dasi, as he thought that the rough life will dissuade her. Parvati was pleased to serve him and stayed with him for many years.

Meanwhile, the gods and people were being terrorised by the demon, Taraka. When they approached Lord Brahma for help, he said that Lord Shiva and Parvati's son will kill the demon. As the gods were getting restless, they decided to help Parvati win Lord Shiva's affection. They sent Lord Kama, the god of love, to Mount Kailash. He saw Parvati at Lord Shiva's feet, sowing a garland. He immediately aimed an arrow at them which struck Lord Shiva.

Lord Shiva opened his eyes and fell in love with Parvati. But he suddenly realised that Lord Kama has played a trick with him. He opened his third eye and burned him to ashes, and banished Parvati from his abode.

Undeterred, Parvati performed severe penance for years. Finally she remembered her previous life and realised that she is none other than the reincarnation of Goddess Sati. When Lord Shiva sensed that as well, he decided to test her.

One day, an old brahmin approached Parvati and asked her, "Why are you performing severe penance, my dear? What do you wish to attain?" Parvati told him about her desire to marry Lord Shiva. The brahmin cringed and asked, "Why would a beautiful maiden like you want to marry someone who covers his body with ash and wears tiger skin?"

Parvati was furious and replied, "What do you know about him? I am the reincarnation of Goddess Sati, his other half. We are incomplete without each other." Suddenly, Lord Shiva revealed his true form to her and consented to marry her.

The gods came down from heaven to attend the grand wedding of Lord Shiva and Goddess Parvati. They retired to Mount Kailash to lead a happy married life.

# THE THIRD EYE

Lord Shiva is known to have an extra eye, on his forehead. But he didn't always have the third eye, it was created. One day, while Lord Shiva was lost in deep meditation, Goddess Parvati decided to play a little game with him. She sneaked up behind him and quickly covered his eyes with her hands. As Lord Shiva could not see anything, the Universe was plunged into complete darkness.

The darkness affected the whole world and it began to crumble and disintegrate. There was great panic all around as no one could do anything to restore the light.

Sensing the chaos in the Universe a third eye suddenly appeared on Lord Shiva's forehead. As he opened it, there was light in the world once again and it was saved from being destroyed.

# SHIVA'S DANCE

Long ago, the sages in Taragam forest performed severe penances to achieve great powers. Soon, they began to think that they were stronger than gods and started creating havoc on earth.

When Lord Shiva heard about them, he appealed to Lord Vishnu and said, "We need to do something to stop them." Lord Vishnu agreed and they made a plan.

Lord Shiva took the form of a young, handsome sage, while Lord Vishnu disguised himself as a beautiful maiden, Mohini. Together, they went to the Taragam forest and approached the sages.

The sages looked at Mohini and immediately fell in love with her dazzling beauty. Their wives were equally enamoured with the young sage. After some time, the sages woke up from their stupor and realised that someone was playing a joke on them. This enraged them immensely and decided to take revenge.

The sages started to perform *yagna*s. The young sage was amused by the turn of events and stood beside them to witness the spectacle. Within moments, an angry tiger leapt out of the fire and pounced on the young sage. But with a smile on his lips, the sage merely grabbed the tiger in mid air and crushed it effortlessly. He ripped off the tiger's skin and placed it around his waist.

The sages could not believe what they saw. Nevertheless, they carried on with their *yagna*, and a fiery serpent sprang out of the fire. The young sage caught the serpent and coiled it around his neck.

Next the sages brought forth an evil demon dwarf, Mulayaka, from the fire. The demon charged at the young sage. Lord Shiva resumed his true form, and without any difficulty, crushed Mulayaka to its death with his feet.

On realising that the rage of the sages is not diminishing, Lord Shiva started dancing, accompanied by celestial music. His enthralling performance pacified the sages, and the world stopped to watch him dance. The beat of his *damru* became the heartbeat of the world, the celestial water flowing from his tresses illuminated his body and his body engulfed the whole cosmos. Such was Lord Shiva's dance that it became symbolic of all the natural laws of the world, expressed beautifully.

# PARVATI AS THE FISHERWOMAN

Lord Shiva, one day decided to tell Goddess Parvati about Brahmadayana, or the mysteries of the Universe. She was very eager to learn, as she knew that only he knew everything about it.

Days turned to months and months to years, and Goddess Parvati listened with unfailing attention, as Lord Shiva expounded the mysteries to her. After several years, there was still no end in sight of Lord Shiva's lessons. Just for a moment, Parvati lost her focus and started admiring the scenery around her.

54

When Lord Shiva noticed that Goddess Parvati was distracted, he became very furious. He yelled, "Ungrateful woman! There are millions who would do anything to hear me speak of Brahmadayana, but you refuse to concentrate. You should be born amongst the fisherfolk so that you learn about hardwork. They know that they cannot afford to think about anything else."

As soon as Lord Shiva uttered those words, poof! Parvati disappeared from his side. Lord Shiva regretted uttering the harsh words. He lamented, "What have I done? How am I supposed to stay happy without you by my side?"

Meanwhile, as Lord Shiva wanted, Goddess Parvati was born as a baby girl on earth. She lay sheltered under a large Punnai tree. When the Chief of the Paravars, a clan of fishermen, found the newborn lying under the tree, he picked her up and said, "The heavens have blessed me! I shall bring her up as my own daughter." He took her to his house, and named her Parvati.

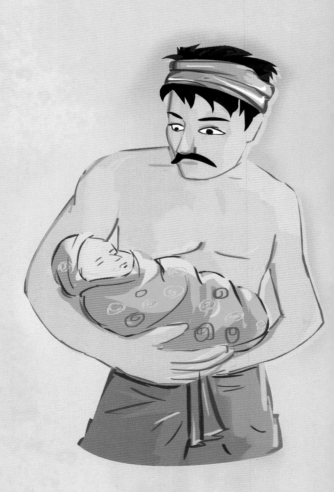

Parvati grew up to a lovely girl, and she was adored by everyone. She would always accompany her father on his fishing expeditions and soon she mastered the art of rowing a boat and also netting the fish in the water.

Lord Shiva was unable to bear the separation from Goddess Parvati and was pining away for her. When Nandi, Lord Shiva's most loyal servant, saw his master in state of despair, he asked "My Lord! Why don't you bring back Goddess Parvati? You know she is living with the Paravars clan. There must be something that you can do to bring her back to Mount Kailash."

"There is nothing I can do," explained Lord Shiva, "As per the law of the world, she will have to marry a fisherman in this birth."

Nandi was adamant to unite his master so he took the form a giant shark and swam to the coast near the Paravars clan. There he saw two fisherman boats and swam towards them. The fishermen panicked on seeing him and tried to row back to the coast, but the shark capsized their boats. For the next few days, Nandi created havoc. He crushed their boats to smithereens, and tore their nets to shreds. He however made sure though that no innocent lives were lost in his quest to return Goddess Parvati to Lord Shiva.

The Chief of the Paravars made an announcement before his people, "I shall give the hand of my daughter to the person who can capture the shark."

Many valiant young men came forward, but Nandi made sure that no one succeeded and continued with his destruction.

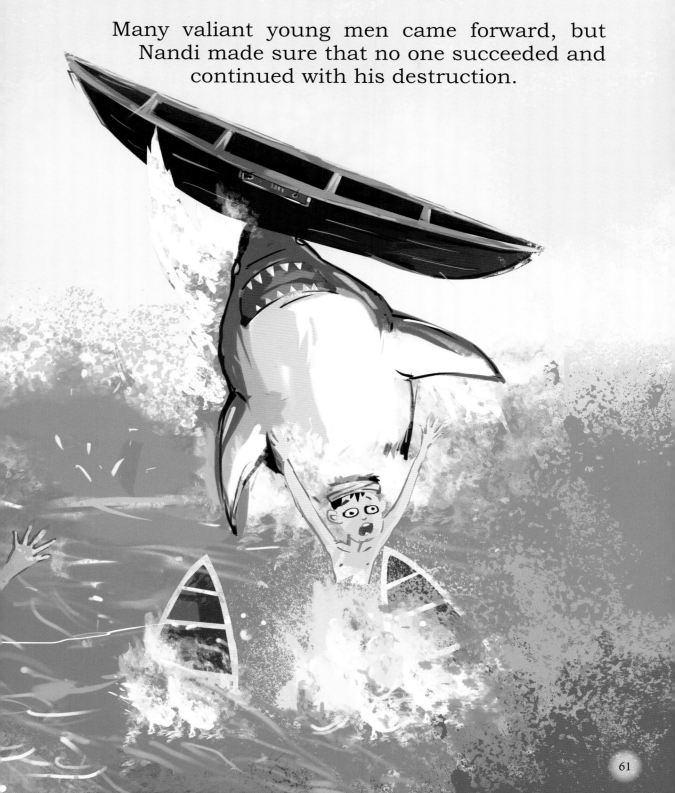

Distraught that no one was able to catch the shark, the Chief along with his daughter started praying to Lord Shiva. Disguising himself as a young fisherman, Shiva approached the Chief.

"I have heard that a shark is bothering you, so I have come to hunt it down."

As the Chief and his fishermen stood by the shores, the young fisherman waded into the water with a net in his hand and caught the giant fish. Nandi recognised his master and allowed him to drag him to the shore.

The clan rejoiced at the end of their troubles and Parvati wedded the young fisherman. After the wedding, Lord Shiva resumed his true form and returned happily to Mount Kailash with his wife.

# ARJUNA'S PENANCE

Mount Indrakila, in the mighty Himalayas, was a tranquil abode to many sages who conducted prayers and performed severe penances to appease the gods.

One day, the sages saw a stranger walking towards their abode. They noticed that even though the stranger was wearing sage's saffron clothes, he looked nothing like one. He was tall, well-built and was carrying weapons. On seeing the golden hilt of the sword, they recognised the stranger to be the Pandava prince, Arjuna.

One of the sages whispered, "The Pandavas were banished from their kingdom, after losing a game of dice with Duryodhana. But what is Prince Arjuna doing here?"

Arjuna walked silently to a secluded spot and sat
down to make a lingam from mud to perform severe
penances to Lord Shiva. He didn't stop his penance
for anything. After a few months, the earth around
him was unable to bear the heat of his penance and
started emanating black smoke around him. The
smoke spread throughout Mount Indrakila, and the
sages fled to Mount Kailash.

They approached Lord Shiva, who was sitting beside Goddess Parvati, and pleaded him to intervene. Lord Shiva smiled and replied, "Please go back to Mount Indrakila. I will resolve your problem."

After the sages left, Lord Shiva could see doubts clouding the Goddess Parvati's' face. He asked her, "What is troubling you? Don't hesitate to ask."

Goddess Parvati asked him, "Why is Arjuna performing such severe penance?" He replied, "Because he wants blessed weapons for the impending war." She still had her doubts and asked, "Do you believe that he will use the weapons wisely and judiciously?" "Well, we will have to find that out," he replied.

Lord Shiva told her about his plan to test Arjuna. He disguised himself as a Kirata Chief (Kirata is a clan of mountain dwellers), and asked Goddess Parvati and some of his followers to dress up as Kirata women.

When they were nearing Mount Indrakila, Goddess Parvati pointed at a wild boar at some distance and said, "That does not look like an ordinary boar." Lord Shiva looked at it and said, "You are right. That looks like the asura, Muka. He seems to heading towards the sages to disrupt their prayers."

Lord Shiva took an aim at the demon with his bow and arrow, but the demon sensed the presence of Lord Shiva and fled. Lord Shiva chased him to the sage's abode, and as soon as the sages saw the boar charging towards them they started running, screaming for help.

Muka ran to the spot where Arjuna was performing his penance. Arjuna sensed the boar's presence and opened his eyes. He took up his bow and arrow to kill it. When Lord Shiva also reached the spot, he said, "Stop! That is my prey. You cannot kill it." Arjuna was not able to recognise Lord Shiva in disguise and replied, "I will not put down my bow. If you are a true hunter take your aim and kill it."

Both shot their arrows at the boar. As soon as arrows pierced, the animal resumed its original demonic self and died. The Kirata women watching the demon fall down to his death, started dancing and celebrating.

But it was not clear who had struck the boar first, and neither party was ready to concede defeat. The Kirata women argued, "He is lying, O Chief! You killed the boar before him." Arjuna did not like to be insulted so challenged the Kirata Chief for a duel.

Soon, arrows started flying between Arjuna and
Lord Shiva. They hurled their best arrows at each
other, but neither of them was hurt. Suddenly, Arjuna
realised that his quiver of arrows was over. Lord Shiva
smiled at him and offered, "You can borrow some
arrows from me." Hearing this, the Kirata women
started mocking Arjuna.

Arjuna angrily threw his bow at the hunter, who caught it, tore the string and flung it away. Not able to control his anger, Arjuna took his sword, and charged him with all his might. The sword dissolved into flowers as it struck the hunter. Everyone was surprised to see the miracle, and the Kirata women cheered their chief.

Refusing to lose, Arjun picked up a tree with his bare hands and hurled it at the hunter, who dodged it easily. Unable to concede defeat, he decided to pray to Lord Shiva for strength. He sat down in front of the lingam and started chanting "Om Namah Shivaya" and placed a garland on the lingam.

Soon, he felt strength infuse his body. Happy that his prayers had been heard, he turned towards the kirata hunter and said, "Lord Shiva had blessed me with strength. Come, let's see who wins now." But as he turned towards the hunter, he saw the garland that he had placed on the lingam was lying around the hunter's neck.

When Arjuna realised that the Kirata Chief was none other than Lord Shiva in disguise, he bowed in front of him and said, "Please pardon me, Lord. I didn't know who I was fighting." Lord Shiva replied, "O valiant prince, you have appease me with your devotion. I grant you this Pashupata, the blessed arrow to aid you in your war."

Years later, during Mahabharata, Arjun used the Pashupata arrow to defeat Karna.

# MARKANDEYA

Sage Mrikandu and his wife Marudvati were devout devotees of Lord Shiva. They were happily married but childless. They decided to perform penance to Lord Shiva to pray for a child.

Impressed by their devotion, Lord Shiva appeared before them and said, "You can ask for anything you want." Mrikandu asked for a child and Marudvati asked for a blessed child. Surprised by the differences in their replies, Lord Shiva smiled and asked, "Do you wish for an ordinary child who will live longer or a gifted child who will live for only sixteen years?"

After a moment's thought, Marudvati replied, "Bless us with a gifted child. Even though he will live for sixteen years, we will have fond memories of him for the rest of our lives." Her husband agreed with her, and Lord Shiva blessed them and disappeared.

In due course, Marudvati gave birth to a son, who was named Markandeya. He grew up to be an exceptionally gifted child. He knew all the Vedas by heart, and mastered Mahamrityunjaya Mantra. The mantra is addressed to Lord Shiva to ward off untimely death or attain immortality.

His parents loved him a lot, but Markandeya sensed a sadness in them. When he asked them about it, Sage Mrikandu told him about the story of his birth. After listening to it, he understood the reason of their sadness. He promised them that he will find a solution to their problem.

As Markandeya's sixteenth birthday approached, his mother was inconsolable. He consoled her and said, "Mother, don't worry. I will pray to Lord Shiva and everything will be fine."

The night he was to turn sixteen, Markandeya started reciting the Mahamrityunjaya Mantra in front of a lingam. The God of Death Yama saw this, but he knew that Markandeya's time on earth was over. He sent two of his servants to bring Markendeya, but the heat emanating from him threw back the servants.

Yama then decided to bring Markandeya himself. When he approached the praying Markandeya, he shook him violently.

Markandeya opened his eyes and pleaded, "I have not finished my prayer to Lord Shiva. Please don't take me away until it's over."

Yama grew impatient and coiled a rope and threw it at Markandeya. The noose fell on Markandeya and the lingam. As Yama tightened the noose, an angry Lord Shiva made an appearance. He struck Yama and killed him. The other gods became very concerned about this. They all approached Lord Shiva and begged him to revive Yama. They explained that without Yama there will be no deaths and people will live for forever, which will create many problems. Lord Shiva relented and revived Yama.

Yama thanked Lord Shiva and enquired about Markandeya, to which Lord Shiva replied, "Markandeya will live forever." Saying so, he blessed the child. As the myth says, Markandeya can still be seen sometimes, trapped in his sixteen years old body, singing the glories of Lord Shiva.

# ANDHAKA

One day Lord Shiva and Goddess Parvati were spending a pleasant day in their abode. Goddess Parvati playfully covered Lord Shiva's eyes with her hands. Suddenly, darkness descended on earth, and her hands started perspiring. The sweat fell on the ground, and a child was born, blind. When Goddess Parvati removed her hands from Lord Shiva's eyes, light was restored on earth.

The couple decided to give the child to Hiranyaksha, a Daitya king, who was childless and was praying for a son. Hiranyaksha adopted the child as his son and named him, Andhaka. When he grew up, he was crowned the king.

Andhakasura, as he came to be known, performed severe penances to Lord Brahma.

Impressed by his devotion, Lord Brahma, asked him, "What do you wish for?" Andhakasura asked him for victories throughout his life and immortality. Lord Brahma granted him the first boon, and added, "I will not be able to grant you immortality as death is inevitable part of life." He instead blessed him that he will die when he will seek the unattainable.

Andhakasura, armed and protected by the blessing of Lord Brahma, raged a vicious war against the gods. The gods were powerless in front of his powers and sought Lord Shiva's help. Lord Shiva, after hearing their pleas, decided to intervene and defeat Andhakasura.

When Andhakasura heard that Lord Shiva had decided to fight in the war, he was enraged. He gathered all his trusted and mighty warriors and sent them to the war. Needless to say, Lord Shiva killed all the demons and proceeded to fight Andhakasura.

Andhakasura and Lord Shiva started fighting, but Andhakasura soon realised that he was no match for Lord Shiva. He fled and hid himself in Goddess Parvati's chambers, with the intention to abduct her and teach Lord Shiva a lesson. This angered Lord Shiva so much that he struck his trident at him. As soon as the blood flowed out of Andhakasura's body and fell on the ground, thousand more demons took birth.

Lord Vishnu was watching the war from a distance. When he saw the situation getting out of hands, he intervened and used his *sudarshan chakra* to kill the demons born out of Andhakasura's blood. Finally, Lord Shiva struck Andhakasura with his trident, and held him up for thousand years. Lord Shiva collected his blood, so as to avoid the birth of more demons from Andhakasura.

After being suspended on Lord Shiva's trident for over thousand years, Andhakasura realised his mistake and sought forgiveness from Lord Shiva. Finally, peace reigned again on earth and the heavens.

# RAVANA'S FOLLY

King Ravana, king of Lanka, was a very devout devotee of Lord Shiva. He would perform many severe penances to appease the Lord.

However, one day he committed a mistake which incurred the Lord's wrath. While meditating at the foothills of Mount Kailash, Ravana felt that he has become stronger than Lord Shiva.

Wanting to test his own strength, Ravana lifted Mount Kailash and placed it on his shoulders. As soon as he did so the mountain started to shake violently.

Lord Shiva then pressed his foot lightly on the mountain and Mount Kailash came tumbling down back to earth, falling completely on Ravana. The King of Lanka had learnt his lesson.

# TRIPURA

After Kartikeya, son of Lord Shiva and Goddess Parvati killed the demon king Taraka, his kingdom fell apart. His sons, Tarakaksha, Vidyunmali and Kamalaksha, began to perform severe penances to appease Lord Brahma. After a few years, a pleased Lord Brahma approached them and said, "Your devotion pleases me immensely. Ask me for any boon you want."

The demons asked him to aid them in building three indestructible cities for them. Lord Brahma replied, "Nothing in this world stays forever. However, the three cities will be safe and strong, and will only be destroyed with one arrow."

The chief architect of the demons, Maya, planned and built the cities. Three floating cities were built — the one on earth was made of iron, the one in the sky was made of silver and the one in heaven had walls made of gold. The three cities were collectively called Tripura.

The three cities would float apart from each other, but once in every thousand years, they would align in a single line with the Pushya star and the moon. This phenomenon would last for only a split second.

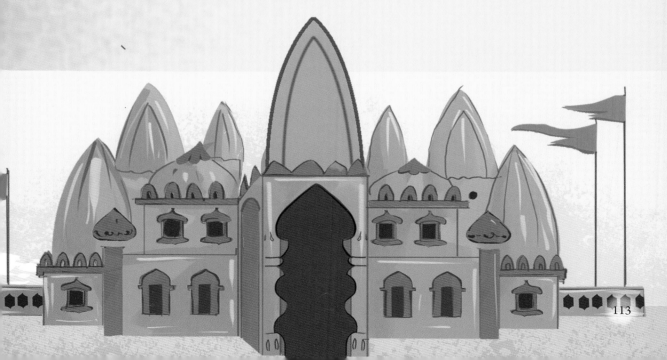

After some time, the demons were not content with living peacefully and decided to lay siege all over the Universe. Maya, sensing the impending doom, started to perform penance to appease the gods. The gods sought Lord Shiva's help in turn. Lord Shiva assured them that he would reduce the three cities to ashes if the demons refused to stop their villainous ways.

Assured that Lord Shiva will fight the demons, the gods attacked the demons with more vigour. So fierce was the fight that the earth slipped from its position and began falling. Lord Vishnu turned into a bull to push back the earth and hold it in its rightful place.

The demons grew very concerned on the day when Lord Shiva was supposed to enter the battlefield. They made several plans to keep him diverted. They knew that if anyone can destroy their cities, it will be Lord Shiva. Lord Shiva finally arrived on the battleground, raised his bow and arrow to strike the cities. The arrow split the three cities in one go, as it was the moment of alignment, reducing Maya's splendid cities to dust and ashes. The demons too perished along with their magnificent cities, finally restoring peace in the Universe.

# SHIVA AS ARDHANARISHVARA

Maharishi Bringi was a devout devotee of Lord Shiva. But he worshipped only the Lord and ignored Goddess Shakti (also known as Goddess Parvati). She was annoyed about it and removed all the energy from the sage's body. As a result, the sage fell on the ground and was unable to move his body. He prayed to Lord Shiva who provided him with a stick to support himself.

Goddess Shakti realised that in order to be worshipped along with Lord Shiva, she had to become an inseparable part of his form. She observed a very strict fast, *kedhara mahavraat*. Impressed by her devotion, Lord Shiva granted her a boon of being one half of his form whereby the Lord appeared on the right side and the goddess on the left side. This form is called Ardhanarishvara, meaning half male and half female.

# SHIVA AS DAKSHINAMURTI

The four sons of Brahma—Sanaka, Sanandana, Sanatana and Sanat—meditated for years, to search for the Supreme Truth, but failed. They finally decided to visit Lord Shiva to seek the answer. They found the Lord sitting in a yoga posture, the Chinmudra posture, under the banyan tree, and sat down around him. Seeing the Lord remain in the same position for a long time, the four sages realised that truth cannot be explained in words and has to be experienced. The form in which Lord Shiva appeared as a Supreme Guide is known as Dakshinamurti—the teacher of all teachers.

# SHIVA AS NEELKANTHA

There was a battle between the gods, and the demons in which, the demons, led by King Bali, won and started ruling the Universe. After being defeated in the battle, the gods lost their powers and energy. They approached Lord Vishnu who advised them to tactfully join hands with the demons and churn the ocean to extract the nectar which will restore their powers and energy. He assured them that he will preside over the event to make sure that the gods receive the nectar.

The ocean was churned using Mount Mandarachala as the churning rod, and Vasuki, the king of serpents, was used as the churning rope. The demons held the head of the snake, while the gods, on the advice of Lord Vishnu, held its tail. The gods and demons pulled back and forth on the snake's body alternately, causing the mountain to rotate, which in turn churned the ocean. However, once the mountain was placed on the bed of the ocean, it began to sink. Vishnu, in his second incarnation as a turtle, Kurma, came to their rescue and supported the mountain on his back.

During the churning of the ocean or *Samudra Manthan*, a dangerous poison, Halahala, emitted from the ocean. This terrified the gods and demons because the poison was so toxic that it would have destroyed all of creation. Lord Vishnu told the gods that only Lord Shiva could save them from the destruction. Lord Shiva on hearing the pleas of the gods decided to swallow the poison. Goddess Parvati panicked, but he assured her that he won't die of the poison. He stored the poison in his throat, which turned blue. Thus Lord Shiva is also known as Neelkantha, the one with blue throat.

# TITLES IN THIS SERIES

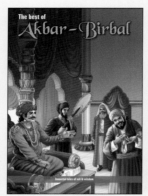

ISBN: 978-93-80069-32-6

ISBN: 978-93-80069-31-9

ISBN: 978-93-80069-33-3

ISBN: 978-93-80070-01-8

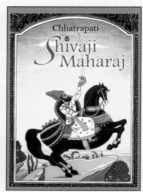

ISBN: 978-93-81607-22-0

ISBN: 978-93-81607-43-5

ISBN: 978-93-81607-34-3

ISBN: 978-93-82607-65-6

ISBN: 978-93-82607-77-9

IBD-A